MRS DELGADO

by Mike Bartlett

Mrs Delgado was first performed at the Old Fire Station, Oxford, on 6 December 2021.

CAST

PERFORMER   Rakhee Sharma

COMPANY

Writer   Mike Bartlett
Director   Clare Lizzimore

Lighting Designer   Rachel Luff
Sound Designer   Jon Ouin
Stage Manager   Tessa Gaukroger
Production Manager   Rachel Luff
Technician   Danny Owen
Technical Assistant   Ben Oakey

Producer   Alexandra Coke
Associate Producer   Will Young

Writing in Isolation

During the national restrictions in 2020 and 2021, I, like many other writers I know, found it hard to actually write. One may have thought, given writers' often-expressed desire to have more solitude to get our work done, this situation would have played to our strengths. Instead, I found it draining, creatively. Of course this was partly because of the anxiety of, and concern for, the situation. But it also made me think about how writers for the theatre are hybrid creatures – half the garret-based social outsider, awkward and anti-social, and half the theatre animal, loving the company of actors and the thrill of collaboration. With that company gone, and the theatres closed, what can a playwright do?

I suppose these two plays are my answer to that question. They were both written during lockdown, with uncertainty about if and when the situation would end, and unsure as to how either of them might be performed. This explains their form. I knew that at the very least they could be short stories. But equally I can tell in the energy of the writing they are designed for performance. The narrator in *Mrs Delgado* is a third character (as revealed in the final line) and the choices they make in how they convey the story reveal them to us. They are also the human being we are physically with in the theatre; watching, and being watched, closely. I write this halfway through rehearsals on the first production at the end of 2021, at the Old Fire Station, Oxford. In that space, this intimate storytelling, without TV or phone screens and completely about *people*, has (as performed by the funny, nuanced and deeply moving actor Rakhee Sharma), become an act of release, defiance and hope.

Phoenix, on the other hand, was performed to its audience during lockdown itself . Through a conversation I was having with the director Sacha Wares, she put me in touch with Richard Twyman at English Touring Theatre. We devised an idea that I would write something that I would perform myself, in an outdoor public space near where I live, in Oxford (this was to be part of the national *Signal Fires* project). Ultimately increased Covid restrictions meant this proved impossible, so as a replacement, I suggested an audio piece, that could use the quiet intimacy of a whispered story, told around a fire. I immediately thought of Bertie Carvel to perform it, and he was captivating, understanding the play required detail, care and absolutely no judgement in performance. That he must just embody the story and character, and let the audience do the work of meaning and morality. It worked fantastically as an audio play. Hopefully one day it will also be performed in person, with a real, present, audience, around a real fire…

Mike Bartlett
November 2021

BIOGRAPHIES

RAKHEE SHARMA | PERFORMER

Rakhee Sharma trained as an actor at The Royal Central School of Speech and Drama. During her training she was awarded the Laurence Olivier Bursary.

Stage credits include: Cathy in *Wuthering Heights* (Royal Exchange Theatre); Fleance and Witch in *Macbeth, If Not Now, When?* (National Theatre, Manchester); *The Last Testament of Lillian Bilocca* (Royal Exchange/Hull Truck) and *Crystal Clear* (Old Red Lion).

TV/film credits include: *Incompatible* (BFI Film); *The Power* (Amazon Original Series) and *The Third Day* (PunchDrunk/HBO).

MIKE BARTLETT | WRITER

Plays for the theatre include: *Vassa* (Almeida Theatre); *Snowflake* (Old Fire Station); *Albion* (Almeida Theatre); *Wild* (Hampstead Theatre); *Game* (Almeida); *King Charles III* (Almeida Theatre/Wyndham's Theatre/Music Box Theatre, New York), *An Intervention* (Paines Plough/Watford); *Bull* (Sheffield Theatres/Off Broadway/Young Vic); *Medea* (Headlong/Glasgow Citizens/Watford/Warwick); *Chariots of Fire* (Hampstead Theatre/Gielgud Theatre); *13* (National Theatre); *Decade* (co-writer Headlong); *Earthquakes in London* (Headlong, National Theatre); *Love,Love,Love* (Paines Plough/Plymouth Theatre Royal/Royal Court/Roundabout Theatre Company, New York); *Cock, Contractions, My Child* (Royal Court Theatre); *Artefacts* (Bush Theatre/Nabokov).

As Director: *Medea* (Headlong/Glasgow Citizens/Watford/Warwick); *Honest* (Theatre Royal Northampton).

Television includes: *Life* (BBC); *Sticks and Stones* (ITV); *Press* (BBC); *Trauma* (ITV); *King Charles III* (Drama Republic/BBC); *Doctor Foster* (Drama Republic/BBC); *The Town* (Big Talk Productions).

CLARE LIZZIMORE | DIRECTOR

Directing includes: *Snowflake*, by Mike Bartlett (Old Fire Station, Oxford/The Kiln, London); *Bull*, by Mike Bartlett (Crucible Studio, Sheffield/59E59, New York/Young Vic, London); *One Day When We Were Young*, by Nick Payne (Paines Plough/Sheffield Theatres/Shoreditch Town Hall); *Lay Down Your Cross*, by Nick Payne, *On the Rocks*, by Amy Rosenthal (Hampstead Theatre); *Pieces of Vincent*, by David Watson (Arcola Theatre); *Faces in the Crowd*, by Leo Butler, *The Mother* by Mark Ravenhill, and *Fear and Misery & War and Peace*, by Mark Ravenhill (Royal Court Theatre); *Jonah and Otto* by Robert Holman (Royal Exchange Theatre, Manchester); *Tom Fool*, by Franz Xaver Kroetz (Citizens Theatre, Glasgow/Bush Theatre) and *The Most Humane Way to Kill a Lobster* by Duncan Macmillan (Theatre503).

As Writer: *Animal* (Atlantic Theatre, New York and Studio Theatre, Washington D.C) and *Mint* (Royal Court). Clare is also under commission with the Royal Court Theatre and Almeida Theatre.

Radio includes: *The Rage* and *Missing in Action* (Both BBC Radio 4).

Awards include: Olivier Award for Outstanding Achievement in an Affiliate Theatre, Channel 4 Theatre Directors Award (formally the RTYDS Award), and the Arts Foundation Theatre Directing Fellowship. Clare has been resident director at Citizens Theatre, Glasgow and a staff director at the National Theatre.

RACHEL LUFF | PRODUCTION MANAGER AND LIGHTING DESIGNER

Lighting design credits include: *Atlantis* (Old Fire Station, Oxford); *A Moment* and *Creating on Borrowed Time* (Thomas Page Dances); *Small Worlds* (The Story Museum); *Contagion Cabaret* (The British Academy and The Pitt Rivers Museum).

JON OUIN | SOUND DESIGNER

Jon Ouin has composed soundtracks for theatre productions including *Mayfly* (Orange Tree Theatre); *Mistero Buffo* (Rhum and Clay) and *Don't Look Away* (Nova Theatre). He has written theme music for recent BBC Radio 4 dramas such as *Undercover Mumbai*, *Someone Dangerous* and *The Chosen One*, as well as for television programmes such as *Catching Britain's Killers* (BBC 2) and *Abducted – Elizabeth I's Child Actors* (BBC Four). Jon was a member of the band Stornoway.

OLD FIRE STATION

The Old Fire Station is a centre for creativity in Oxford housing two organisations: the homelessness charity Crisis and an arts centre. We share our building. We encourage people from all backgrounds to understand and shape the world in which we live through stories, creativity and the arts, and by connecting with others.

ART IS FOR EVERYONE. EVERYONE HAS POTENTIAL.

WHAT WE DO

Produce and present across art forms

We want our reputation to be good quality art, in person and online, which is aimed at adults, takes a risk, asks questions and entertains. We want our audiences to have fun and be open to new ideas and different people.

Help people to be creative

We want people to be able to write, sing, draw, devise, design, perform, move, make, imagine, play and create – physically and online – individually or with others and to a high standard. Creativity includes artistic practice but also extends to technology and science and imaginative thinking. We want people to tell their own stories using the medium that works best for them.

Support artists

We want early to mid-career artists from all disciplines to have access to the advice, networks and promotion they need to develop their practice as creatives and as facilitators of other people's creativity.

Include people facing tough times because of disadvantage

We share our building with the homelessness charity, Crisis. Through this partnership, we offer people who are homeless space to define themselves and choose their own labels by including them in the running of the centre. We also seek to include others who are socially isolated and disadvantaged. We do not focus on homelessness. We focus on what people who face disadvantage can offer.

Work with communities across Oxford

With Crisis, we offer a public space which is shared by very different people and helps to break down barriers and promote solidarity in Oxford. We also work through partnerships beyond our building with different communities around Oxford.

WHAT WE CONSIDER IN EVERYTHING WE DO

Face the climate emergency

This means working with others to

- educate ourselves about the emergency,
- take practical steps to reduce carbon emissions,
- use our creativity to help our community face the challenges ahead.

Unlearn discrimination

This means working with others to

- educate ourselves about racism and other forms of discrimination in cultural organisations (especially with regards to disability and class),
- take practical steps to become more representative of diverse communities,
- use our creativity to explore diverse culture and challenge ignorance or abuse.

Be human friendly

This means working with others to

- educate ourselves about healthy organisational culture and decision making,
- take practical steps to develop honest supportive relationships within our team, with our volunteers, our partners and funders and with the public,
- use our creativity to promote services founded on good quality relationships and learning.

It also means having fun!

Experiment and listen

To make great art and to achieve change we need to experiment and play.

This means taking risks, being prepared to fail and being able to adapt and respond. It also means listening carefully to those with whom we work, reflecting deeply on what we do and how we do it, and measuring impact primarily through storytelling.

Build financial resilience

This means ensuring that we are here for the long term by diversifying income streams, securing core and project funding, developing the business and minimising expenditure whilst delivering our mission and maintaining appropriate levels of reserves. It also means ensuring that those we work with are properly paid to help them become financially resilient.

HOW DO WE DO IT?

We do all this by focusing on:

- good quality relationships
- listening and learning
- encouraging creativity and risk-taking
- offering a public space which is welcoming to all
- working collaboratively online, outside and elsewhere

Why is this needed?

Oxford is globally renowned for stunning heritage and outstanding research.

Oxford is also a place of disadvantage and inequality.

Oxford needs the Old Fire Station because it is about openness, inclusion, looking forward and different thinking.

The Old Fire Station acts as a bridge between sectors, organisations and people.

www.oldfirestation.org.uk

OLD FIRE STATION

Our thanks to Windich Legal for supporting *Mrs Delgado*.

MRS DELGADO

Note on Text

(–) means the next line interrupts.

(…) at the end of a speech means it trails off. On its own it indicates a pressure, expectation or desire to speak.

A line with no full stop at the end indicates that the next speech follows on immediately.

Dialogue in brackets indicates the point being made is parenthetical to the main argument.

This text went to press before the end of rehearsals and so may differ slightly from the play as performed.

ONE

There was something almost supernatural about Mrs Delgado, Helen thought, as she stared out her back window at the house opposite, while stirring her cup of tea with a Sainsbury's own-brand chocolate bourbon. Helen liked the idea of the supernatural. In fact she wished the supernatural happened more often. It seemed to her that given the number of supernatural occurrences that appeared in fiction, the amount that happened in real life was... well... dispiriting. She remembered clearly at breakfast, aged four, when her mother explained in astonishingly plain language that the tooth fairy was entirely made up. That getting money for discarded body parts was a gruesome idea and wasn't going to happen, not just because fairies didn't exist but because the source of the cash, her, was broke. From then onwards the following twenty-eight years had been a process of lowering expectations. All possible avenues for the supernatural had one by one, been closed off: Father Christmas was an early casualty. Loch Ness has been scanned by lasers and found to be empty. They'd worked out how the Egyptians had built the pyramids and it turned out they didn't use aliens, just physics. Even Derek Acorah turned out to be a fraud. And then died. Yes, she thought as the wet bourbon collapsed under the sheer weight of tea, the world had proved to be obstinately natural and consistently not-super.

Especially this year.

Mrs Delgado was, from what she could tell, pruning a house plant. Incredibly slowly.

Helen glanced down at an Amazon parcel by the door, still not disinfected. Recent reports were that the virus could survive on surfaces for twenty-eight days. That was a longer lifespan than any of her previous three relationships. Although the most recent 'relationship' maybe shouldn't count since it was one night, entirely about sex, and sex that didn't even happen. His name was Mark. They had met on Tinder and agreed a date. It had got off to a bad start when the restaurant had failed to receive her booking, and had no space. Her flat was just round the corner so they had gone back there, where one thing (him coming in) had very quickly led to another (him taking his top off). It was then awkward as she faced a moral dilemma. He was very attractive. He had muscles on his arms just the right size, like they came from genetic and accidental athleticism, not hours in the gym. Helen liked this. He also was quite lean and looked like he was ready to just sort of... go to town on her. He seemed adept, liberal, and generous. Like he was a man into actual real-life actual women who had bits and hair and fluids and needs. It was a guess of course but she was good at judging these things and so, in conclusion, yeah, she was definitely up for it.

Technically. Because unfortunately, unlike Mark, she'd not prepared for actual sex to be on the cards on this very first date and she hadn't thought it through. Once he started coming on to her, moving closer, she had got flustered, at first found excuses to move away like, 'Oh actually have you seen this weird shape in the wall?' or 'Actually shall I close the blind, we don't want people looking in do we?' but eventually that strategy had become exhausted and she had to stop him and say look, sorry, sorry, this kind of casual sexual encounter? Would you believe it's actually against the rules?

We're not allowed. Because of the old... You know, corona.

She smiled.

Then apologised. She was desperately sorry – really – but a quick fuck wasn't going to be possible, not right now. Maybe next year? He was stopped in his tracks. He looked... bewildered and hurt and then looked up at her like she was some kind of weirdo.

But she wasn't, was she? These were the rules. And they had quite a lot of moral weight behind them. I mean if they did it, they could literally accidentally kill someone.

He didn't reply. So almost just to fill the silence Helen said politely that the only thing she could suggest is if what if perhaps they were to get themselves off, while looking at the other person? That might be... well... A reasonable socially distanced option? (She didn't in fact want to do it as she sensed correctly that it had a very high risk of being awful and literally anticlimactic but she felt she had to show some kind of willing and maybe if he removed his top and those arms of his were involved she might find a way to get over the line or at the very least convincingly pretend.)

'Nah.' He said. 'Maybe just call it a night.'

She agreed and in seconds he was on his way and out the door.

She didn't regret it. It was that kind of bending of the rules she hated. People thinking that a small misdemeanor might not matter very much, without realising that if everyone does it, the minor becomes the major and starts to matter a hell of a lot. The cost would be counted in lives. She had to hold the line: No sex. No thank you. Not with strangers. She's making a stand against the global pandemic by not putting out. We all have to make sacrifices. And hers was whatever Mark would have done to her with his lean toned body and care and strength and, probably, eventually, penis. That would all have to remain a really quite frustrating mystery.

But yes. Twenty-eight days. And yes, the biscuit was history, a mush at the bottom of the mug. And no. There was no such thing as the supernatural.

Except, possibly, for this old woman opposite.

Mrs Delgado.

Perhaps she was the exception.

Mrs D snipped the house plant and it collapsed. Not simply a branch but the entire thing, just fell, inelegantly, to the floor. The woman stared at it for a moment, then abandoning all care, picked the whole thing up and dumped it in her kitchen bin.

Helen always liked watching Mrs Delgado. There was always a new piece of madness. Helen had at first tried not to look:

to respect the unspoken rule in a city that although one happened to be able to see in at each other's windows, one never *watched*. But the problem was that every time Helen opened the blind on her back window Mrs Delgado was doing something really weird. Smoking a very long thin cigarette while sat on the kitchen table. Standing in her small garden hanging up washing that was all, every bit of it, made of wool. Or just standing in the living room staring straight up, for four minutes. Of course this year there had been more opportunity for this observation than previously and it turned out Mrs Delgado's madness was daily. She knew who Helen was well enough to wave if she saw her. Occasionally they would smile if they passed in the street, but really, other than these sporadic acts of mild eccentricity Helen knew very little about her.

The old woman turned away from the house plant. She seemed to hear a noise and she rushed out of the room. A few moments later she came out the back door. Just as she did a young man came through the gate that opened into her back garden from the side passage. The man was maybe forty with long greying hair in a ponytail. He was unshaven and had the impression he needed someone in his life to care for him. He shuffled into the garden, and saw Mrs Delgado. They spoke (Helen couldn't hear what about. She was too far away and her window was closed).

At first they observed social distancing rules quite well. But then Mrs Delgado looked concerned and after a minute or two the man became upset. He was standing facing away from Helen but from his shoulders, which tensed and then started shaking, she knew he was crying. She saw Mrs Delgado watch, then put down the secateurs which were still in her hand, and walk over to the man, whom Helen now felt sure was probably her son. She got closer and closer. Then she reached out and hugged him. Tightly. He relaxed in the hug and sobbed. Really hard. Then she kissed his head. A moment. Then they broke and he quickly stood back. Helen knew he was saying they shouldn't have hugged but Mrs Delgado shrugged and suddenly looked full of – like there was a flash of something in her eyes – she looked sharp, forceful and like a young woman, just for a second. She said something certain and defiant.

They spoke for a few minutes, then the son left. Mrs Delgado went back inside.

It was a touching scene. But Helen was concerned. This woman must have been mid-eighties, at least. If she got corona she'd have a twenty-something per cent chance of dying from it. She had been reckless to hug her son. Yes he was upset and it was tough but there were people in that situation all over the country who had resisted. Her son had been reckless too, to allow it. Still, nothing to be done now. Helen carried on with her day, moved on, but a note had been made. And almost unintentionally, each day, when she could, she kept an eye out, just looking, out the window, at this impulsive old lady.

And what she saw, shocked her to her core.

TWO

Over the next week, Mrs Delgado received fifteen visitors.
This included people delivering shopping, a few friends, some
other individuals who were probably family, a nurse, an
Amazon delivery person who was persuaded in for a cup of tea
somehow, and a man who Helen thought was probably there to
deal with some damp. Mrs Delgado had failed to properly
socially distance from every single one of these fifteen people.
Ten of them she hugged, including, oddly, the Amazon guy.
Seven of them she kissed on the cheek.

Helen could be sure of these statistics as she'd been keeping
notes. And of course she was aware that there were probably
more than fifteen. She had been out a few times – met a couple
of people for walks, had a day trip to see her mum. And of
course she wasn't watching literally every second of the day.
One could probably take that number of fifteen encounters and
double it. So Mrs Delgado had put herself in danger thirty times
this week. Thirty opportunities where she might easily catch a
virus which could kill her. And it was so strange that with so
many of them it wasn't just standing too close, it was proper
2019 physical affection. She clearly had a manner which took
people by surprise when she went for it in this way, and they
didn't feel quite able to stop her.

Helen had met people like this and even before the virus, she
hated it. Being forced into a physical relationship with
someone, hugging after you've met them once, kissing on the
cheek as a greeting. It had always been ridiculous and a silver
lining of 2020 had been that disappearing, hopefully forever.
But Mrs Delgado seemed to be throwing caution, and public
health, to the wind. After this had happened five or six times
Helen had decided that she must have a death wish. It was the
only explanation. She must know the risks but actually wanted
to catch it. She'd had enough of life and was actively seeking
the Reaper to come and mow her fucking down.

It was like watching someone teetering on the edge of a high building, or bridge, about to jump. The right ethical thing to do was to intervene, for their own good. Morally there was no question. It had been a week. That was long enough. It was time, Helen decided in her head, to act.

So on Tuesday afternoon she was stood on Mrs Delgado's doorstep wearing her transparent visor (she guessed Mrs Delgado might have some trouble hearing so having her lips visible was considerate), and having just antibacced her hands, she rang the bell and took a big step back.

There was a moment and then the door opened. Mrs D was wearing a red flowing outfit and a flower in her matted hair. She looked bohemian and completely card-carrying crazy.

'Hello' she said.

'Hi I'm Helen' said Helen, 'I live opposite, we've met a couple of times'

'Oh yes, that's right I know, you live on your own'

'Yes.'

'You have men round sometimes'

'I…well…'

'You don't always pull the curtains fully closed in your bedroom'

'There's a blind.'

'It's transparent'

'Er no the label said translucent but – '

'You can see all the way through it darling.'

'Oh.'

'Yes.'

'…'

'But don't be concerned I never got kicks from watching other people fucking – too busy doing it myself or used to be those were the days but yes it certainly means I feel you and I happen to share some... intimacy.'

Mrs Delgado looked at her, without a smile. Helen was... taken aback. This old woman had seen her naked. She's potentially seen... well... quite a lot of things. Images went through her head. The possible... activities Mrs Delgado had observed...

'Alright?' interrupted the older woman.

'Yes. I... sorry' said Helen, coming back to the moment 'I er... I wanted to come over as I've noticed that... well I can see you from my kitchen and I've noticed that when you have visitors you're not socially distancing from them.'

Mrs Delgado looked at her. Quizzical. But she didn't say anything. Helen continued.

'And I know really it's not my business but on the few occasions we've spoken I liked you and I don't want to see you getting the virus and... getting ill so I wanted to make sure you knew the rules and if you needed any help or anything?'

Helen smiled. She had decided in advance to phrase it like this. As an offer of assistance rather than a rebuke. She felt it would be more likely to be accepted. Mrs Delgado watched her for a second.

'You want to come in?'

'Oh. No thank you.' (She should have stopped there but she couldn't help herself adding...) 'Not a good idea.'

'Right.'

Mrs D looked at Helen again, then without saying anything, reached for a bureau just by the door. From it she produced a packet of Camel cigarettes and a small black lighter. She neatly took out a single fag, put it into her mouth and lit it. She blew the smoke away from Helen, but Helen could still smell it. Made her realise how many of these particles we absorb all the time, from strangers' mouths and lungs, into our own...

Mrs Delgado stared at Helen, standing there, at a distance, in her plastic visor. Helen felt like she was an alien visiting from another world. The way Mrs Delgado looked at her wasn't, as one might expect, judgemental. Or critical. It was… well… she looked interested.

'I know the rules' she said.

'Good. I just. I'd hate to see you get ill.'

'You don't know me'

'No but just… I'd hate anyone to get ill.'

'Everyone gets ill.'

A trace of frustration in Helen that she tried and failed to hide.

'Of course. I mean dangerously ill.'

'Everyone gets dangerously ill. Eventually, one way or another'

'Yes but – '

'You're worried I might die'

'Exactly.'

'Well I am going to die. Before too long. Certain of that sweetheart. Been smoking since I was fifteen. I'm eighty-seven now.'

'You mean you're ill… like terminally?' Helen had wondered this. Whether Mrs Delgado had nothing to lose.

'Oh! No. Every time I go to the doctor's they say I'm astonishingly well.'

'Then why take the risk?'

'Yes. Why? Why would I do that?'

She looked at Helen as if the answer was obvious or about to suddenly appear. Like riddle-me-fucking ree. Like Helen was Sarah in *Labyrinth* and Mrs Delgado was a Jim Henson puppet, offering a riddle. But Helen had had enough of this. She wasn't bloody… Sarah. And Mrs Delgado wasn't a latex puppet. Despite appearances. No. This was serious.

'It's not just you, it's transmission to other people. Even if you don't care about yourself, it's not responsible.'

'Really...' said the old woman with a little smile.

'Yes!' said Helen, pissed off at being patronised and now getting into her stride. 'And I know this bohemian smoking don't-give-a-fuck attitude has got you a long way in life, I know you've probably had an amazing time carpe-dieming to the max – '

'Yes I have,' interrupted Mrs Delgado.

'...Yes, but that attitude of being entirely about you and being liberal and libertarian and rule-breaking and funny and taboo-busting doesn't work any more. That attitude is going to kill people. I'm sorry but I see it all the time. People like you they think they can duck and dive past the virus, that it won't get them and that everyone's exaggerating the dangers but fifty thousand people have died of it already in this country alone. And they might be old or have health conditions but every one of them is a person with friends and family, every one of them is just as important as you.'

'What's the matter?' asked Mrs Delgado, softly.

'What?!' said Helen.

'You're not happy.'

Helen looked at her, offended. And confused. And surprised. And annoyingly, right in this second, without an answer. She WAS happy. She was absolutely fucking content actually, she thought, but if she said that out loud it would obviously sound like she was protesting too much and prove the opposite. So...

A moment where she considered her options.

Then she finished the conversation.

'Look I've done what I can. I would just ask that you did your bit.'

And she turned and left. 'Did your bit' sounded a bit rhetorical but perhaps it would appeal to a wartime instinct or something that might be lurking in this pensioner. Although Helen actually knew she was less forties-influenced than sixties. That was the problem. She was a fucking hippy. If only we had a post-war-resilient-public-minded generation still going. Instead we've got a bunch of pampered *Daily Mail*-reading fucking ageing dropouts. As she walked away she heard behind her:

'If you want to come and have a cup of tea darling you're more than welcome. If you ever want to talk.'

She stopped for a second, considering a reply, then walked on. 'Talk.' What an obvious passive-aggressive move. Inviting her in. The exact opposite of the point she was making. Ignore it. Ignore this lady. Fine. Just... Let her die. Let her simply fucking die.

THREE

And that was the plan: Ignore Mrs Delgado. Let Delgado die. But she couldn't. Because the visitors kept coming. All different sorts, and Helen realised she was the only one who knew, probably, the number of different people coming in, and how Mrs D treated them all like this. They probably thought it was only them but no, this was consistent behaviour, and Helen was the only witness. She started to feel the responsibility, not just to Mrs Delgado herself but to the community. If this old woman got it and didn't realise for five days or whatever that would be over thirty people she would pass it on to, who might then spread it in turn. Helen considered calling the police, then decided it was unlikely that

a) they would do anything.

b) Mrs Delgado would listen to them even if they spoke to her.

and c) there was a chance, if provoked, that Mrs Delgado might mention seeing some regular recreational drug use that may have happened behind the now apparently transparent blind a few years ago.

Therefore Helen decided instead to become a very very low-level vigilante.

From the back window of her flat she could see people approaching Mrs D's front door. People would turn the corner and head for either her house or the one adjacent. It would take them about thirty seconds from when she first saw them to ringing the doorbell. She had timed this. It took her twenty-eight seconds to get out of her flat, down the stairs and to the corner where she could call to them. All this she had practised. So she waited, shoes on, key in her pocket. Not sat there – that would make her feel stupid – but aware, as she did chores in the house, that she was looking out of the window a lot. Then she saw him, a delivery guy, the Amazon guy, the same one. He'd appeared

round the corner with yet another parcel. Helen shot out her door,
leapt down the steps three at a time ran out her front door, zipped
to the left around the corner and immediately shouted 'hey!' She
caught the delivery man just in time. He was about to ring the
bell but looked up, surprised. From the expression on his face he
seemed as if he feared physical assault, and Helen was aware that
she was still travelling at some speed, so now he had paused, she
downshifted to a trot and although out of breath and full of
adrenaline, attempted a smile.

'Sorry... just...' But she couldn't continue. She was breathing
too heavily. She held up her hand indicating him to wait as she
walked towards him. He stood, holding the parcel, now irritated
rather than frightened. Helen remembered that these delivery
guys are up against the clock, if they didn't squeeze in exactly
the right deliveries at the right time, they'd miss out. No time
for chat or toilet breaks. Terrible job really. Anyway, she finally
arrived two metres away from him, swallowed, exhaled and
explained herself.

'I needed to talk to you about the lady in there. She – '

'Mrs Delgado.' He interrupted.

'Yes,' said Helen, 'now she's... lovely, very nice but she doesn't
seem to understand social distancing. Last time you were here
I saw you go inside – '

'She's lonely.'

'She – right, yes – '

'She told me she was lonely and could do with a chat, and
you know I can't really afford to do that but the way things are
I figured there's nothing more important, than looking after
someone who – '

'Well that's it really.' Helen smiled again. Again here was
someone who didn't understand. Who was living in a different
time. Did none of these people watch the news? Or *read* the
news? Or listen to all the fucking *news*, or just own a smartphone.
The endlesss endless reporting on this virus and the endless
playschool level of messaging about the importance of distance

and isolation from each other. The idea that going into her home
and having a cup of tea with her and letting her hug him was
LOOKING AFTER HER. I mean it was either stupid or... well
no. It was just stupid. Again she tried not to show this.

'That's it. By going in, you're not looking after her. You're
having contact with lots of people every day. And if you go
inside, she's old and could get the virus and she could die and
neither of us wants that.'

'She could die of loneliness'

'Well. Yes. I know that is true, but to be blunt. Not as quickly.'

The delivery driver looked at her. He had an answer to this
clearly. Helen had said it firmly and decisively but in the short
silence that followed she saw he wasn't going to waste any
more of his time discussing it.

'So what do you want me to do?'

'Just leave the parcel on the doorstep, then go. I'll ring the
doorbell once you're far enough away, and then leave her to
pick it up. Completely contactless.'

He took a last look at the door, then gave her the parcel and
walked away, back to his van. She waited a moment, as
promised, then like a schoolboy game of postman's knock, she
put the parcel down on the ground, rang the old woman's bell
and then ran, literally ran away. She didn't want a conversation
with her, to explain why she was there. She didn't even want to
be seen. She got round the corner and went back up to her flat.
From her window she saw Mrs Delgado come back into the
kitchen having collected the parcel. She opened it. It was a
multipack of Rizla papers. Mrs Delgado sat down at the table
and began to roll a cigarette, slowly. Once done, she lit it, and
sat alone, smoking.

Helen stood looking at her. Then pulled down the new blind.
Two days ago she had replaced it. This once was solid. Ikea.
Who now, at last, did delivery. Admittedly no light could get
through, but no one could see in either. Much better.

Over the next two weeks Helen kept a look out for deliveries to
Mrs Delgado's house, and by her reckoning, was intercepting
about seventy per cent. She probably missed some. And there
were a couple she had thought might have been too awkward to
stop – Like that long-haired man in his forties, the one who was
probably the son – he seemed happier now. But if seventy per
cent was even nearly accurate, that was a huge reduction. She
was proud of that. And contrary to the concern of the Amazon
man, Mrs Delgado seemed in good spirits, continuing with her
daily regime of total insanity.

Also, as the days went on, Helen's work was getting less
onerous as a number of people were repeat customers, who had
got the message and now left the parcel, rang the bell and made
a quick retreat. So it was only the occasional new face that
meant Helen had to do the dash to get to them. One had been a
plumber, and of course Helen couldn't stop him going in, if he
was genuinely needed, but she asked him to wear his mask and
his visor, to not get into any real conversation, to avoid being
too close to her, and to finish up as quickly as possible. He
made Helen a promise, and from what she could see from her
window, was very professional. Sure enough he'd got out of
there quickly.

So this was success. Helen had brought the risk down. Now it
was manageable, and Mrs Delgado had a much greater chance
of getting through this. Would she ever know, that this woman
she probably hated, was actually saving her life?

Helen was pondering all this, as she opened the plastic
wrapping on a Sainsbury's mackerel salad. She didn't really
want a salad. She wanted to heat up the three slices of leftover
Papa John's in the fridge. But she was aware she was heavier
than she should be, and weight was one of the key risk factors.
So the pizza was rejected. For now. Perhaps it would be dinner.
Or a snack this afternoon. Helen took the salad into the living
room, put the news channel on and sat down. She was about to
eat, when the buzzer went. There was a moment when she
thought she might ignore it, but she was waiting for a delivery
of some Nespresso coffee pods and didn't want them to take

them away, thinking she wasn't in, so she jumped up and grabbed the intercom phone.

'Hello'

'It's April'

'It's…'

Helen was confused. It was September.

'Sorry…?'

'April Delgado. Your neighbour.'

'Oh. Right…'

'I need to speak to you. Can I come in?'

Blood rushed to Helen's face. What was this woman doing? This was outrageous. Aggressive.

'Well, no I don't think that's a good idea. What's it about?'

This was disingenuous and Helen knew it. She could guess why April Delgado had come to see her. The plumber probably told her about the strange lady coming up to him on the doorstep. April Delgado was here to tell Helen where she could proverbially go.

'I've got something for you,' she said.

'Oh. You mean…'

'A little something. To say thank you. For your concern'

Helen was cautious, and deeply aware of the madness that could take this lady over. The 'something' could be a knife. A rat in a bag. A spit in the face. Yes, that would be exactly a punishment this lady would find suited her crime – the moment Helen opened the door, she would expectorate nastily to give Helen the virus through her actual bile.

'Oh that's sweet of you. Maybe can you leave it on the doorstep?'

'No I don't really want to do that. Could you come down and collect it?'

Like everyone who had grown up in this country Helen was
aware of the power of embarrassment and politeness. It was
strong. The fear of upsetting someone, causing a scene, or
seeming 'weird', was enough to make you do the strangest
things. She had read of people being inhibited from shouting
'help' when drowning, simply because it felt ridiculous. She'd
had friends who had been in hospital having just given birth,
and had midwives insult them, take their babies away, shove
them around, making mother and baby cry and say nothing in
protest simply because of this weird British trait. Helen was
fully aware it was better to state the truth, say what you wanted
calmly and factually and that actually, most of the time people
appreciated that. So in this instance, where she knew the old
lady was engaged in a power play to get her to come downstairs
in person, she should simply say 'I'm so sorry I don't feel
comfortable with that. If you can leave it on the step that would
be much better for me.' But for some reason, almost
instinctively, she found herself using a soft high-pitched voice
and saying 'Alright! Be down in a second.' She winced at her
own weakness, then hung up the intercom phone, ran to the
kitchen, put on her mask, squirted some Boots sanitiser on her
hands, rubbed it in, grabbed her key, opened the door and went
down into the hall.

Once there she could see a figure through the frosted glass on
the main door to the building. This interaction was clearly
hotting up. Helen had never intended to get involved like
this – certainly not in a way that would produce confrontation.
A friend of hers, Chris, had someone stalk him for ten years.
It ruined his life.

She braced herself, opened the door, then took a big step back.
Mrs Delgado was stood, holding a large plastic box. She smiled.

'For you'

'Oh'

'It's a fruit cake'

'Right'

'With mango.'

'Mango?'

'I used dried mango. I don't know if it'll work but it's what I had and there's no reason it shouldn't.'

'Right.'

A moment where Helen wasn't sure if she was missing something. Some implication. But she couldn't leave the cake hanging there. She took it, and held it, consciously thinking that she mustn't touch her eyes, nose or mouth till the plastic box was upstairs in quarantine and she'd managed to wash her hands.

'I know you think you're doing the right thing,' continued Mrs Delgado. 'And I appreciate it, but now, please, it's time to stop.'

She was serious in a way she hadn't been before. But this drew out a similar conviction in Helen.

'I'll stop when you stick to the rules.'

'That's up to me'

'Well no, actually'

'My choices'

'Yes but'

'My business'

'It's everyone's business. It affects everyone.'

Mrs Delgado didn't reply. Just looked at her.

'I know it seems hard. But – '

'You're interfering'

'Everyone says if you see people not following the rules then – '

'You don't have many friends.'

'I'm... what?'

'You have one good friend. But you don't see many people. And you have occasional men up here but you've not had a proper relationship, not in the five years since you moved in.'

'Look – '

'But you want one. You're desperate for love, essentially, aren't you, and you don't have it, and that makes you sad at night, very sad, which is why you eat, why you take those drugs.'

'Have you finished?'

'And why you're doing this to me. You're always on your phone, I see you, all the time, head down, but you don't have anyone in your life and you feel bad about that, so all these rules they're exactly what you want. You think I've got no one and neither should anyone else.'

'Wow. Okay – '

'But it's not very nice.'

'It's not about… nice. It's just wanting you to – '

Helen stopped, as she said those last few words her voice was breaking. Wavering. Oh god. She was – she couldn't – She used her elbow to shut the door. Essentially in Mrs Delgado's face. And there she was, in the hall, holding the plastic box. This crazy woman's fucking *cake*.

She had no right. No right to say… any of it.

She glanced and could see, through the glass, the shape still there for a moment. Maybe thinking Helen might open the door again. She looked at this plastic box. It was… contaminated. Probably. She put it down on the floor. She was crying but that was –

She wiped the tears away. Then stood up and suddenly opened the door. Mrs Delgado had just turned to go. Now she turned back. Took in Helen.

'I don't want to upset you. Why can't we just – '

'Take it back.'

'You mean?'

Helen looked down at the box on the floor. Who put mango in a fruit cake fucking anyway? Mrs Delgado looked at Helen and the cake.

'It was for you. I wanted you to know that you're not on your own, actually. That people do look out for you. We all do. The street. The community'

'Community? There isn't a fucking – '

'Yes. Haven't you noticed?'

Helen swallowed. Stayed on target.

'If you don't take it back it'll just… remain… here, on the doorstep. I don't want it.'

Mrs Delgado looked a little unsure.

'Helen, I know you mean well but it's important that you let me do things my own way. Alright?'

'But we're not separate people. That's what you don't understand. Everyone is connected whether they like it or not. We all have a responsibility. To each other. I'm taking that responsibility. You're not.'

'You really feel connected Helen?'

'I… it's not about how I *feel*. You're not allowed to see people. You're not *allowed*. Do you understand? Have you noticed that? On the news? I know it's unusual but right now, for your own good, for everyone's good, I'm sorry, but it's the fucking… rule.'

A moment, then April Delgado bent down, dignified, picked up the plastic box, turned and walked down the street, alone, back to her house.

Helen closed the door.

FOUR

Helen was very pleased with her new, solid, light-impermeable Ikea blind. In fact she now had four of them, as she had taken no chances and replaced every blind she owned. In true lockdown spirit, she'd done the work herself and with the exception of the one in the living room which was slightly drooping on the left-hand side, she was proud. The only thing was that during waking hours Helen now faced a binary choice. Either she opened the blind, meaning she got light, but then everyone, anyone, could see in completely. Or she closed it, but that meant it was pitch black and she needed the overhead lights on, which made the flat feel like a bunker.

Like she was hiding.

Which she wasn't.

She had no reason to.

It was true she had certainly had enough of Mrs Delgado. She'd tried her best, and all she'd got back was a character assassination. Which was pretty typical of that kind of manipulative person. She had *friends*. Mrs Delgado was such a… Of course she had *friends*. She was fine.

Absolutely fine.

Absolutely fine.

She reached into the fridge and retrieved a packet of crumpets for her elevenses. She'd done a Zoom with her manager, who'd spent more time talking about her jumper and virtual backgrounds than what they were supposed to be discussing. through Helen had decided that if she could get through the call without being rude, she'd treat herself to a Sainsbury's crumpet with Marmite, and ten minutes of Phil and Holly, before getting back to work. Having got the food from the fridge, she went to put the blind up but at the last minute decided against it. She was just not keen for that woman to look and see her in the kitchen. It would seem to confirm that Helen was comfort eating, which, again, was not right.

It had been a week since the encounter at the door. She hadn't seen Mrs Delgado since then. Mainly because, if she was honest, once the blinds had been fitted, they'd been down seventy per cent of the time.

Maybe eighty per cent.

She glanced at the post on the side, that she'd got from the front door earlier. It was the usual collection of junk mail. She was about to ignore it when she spotted, sticking out of the side, a bright-green, home-made... flyer... thing, written in felt tip. Intrigued, she fished it out.

'Doorstep Street Party! This Friday 15th. 7 p.m. Come together, best we can. Bring food and drink. We'll have music, entertainment, and dance the evening away. All from the comfort of your doorstep. Everyone welcome.'

And then the shocker.

'For more information, or to provide entertainment, contact Mrs April Delgado, number 25.'

Right.

Now.

Helen had lived on the street six years and no one had ever felt the need to have a party before. Indeed there hadn't been so much as Neighbourhood Watch. Now, she mused, the one moment we're all supposed to be keeping our distance, Mrs Delgado decides, on her own, that it's time to have a boozy old knees-up. She's been informed, probably by her son, that she has to tell people to stay on their doorsteps, but honestly after a few beers how long will that last? Helen didn't want to be miserable about this. And she didn't want to make it personal but she couldn't help thinking what a strange *coincidence* it was that Mrs Delgado had *suddenly* decided to become a community organiser a week after they'd got into their dispute...

She'd talked about community, hadn't she?

This was another power play. An attempt to make her point.

It's sad, Helen thought, as not many people are actually going to take part. The street wasn't close. A lot of the flats were short-term rents, young people who had their own groups of friends, some older professionals who had a house in the country and a flat here as their whatever. So there wasn't much to link people, no one spoke, and for the past six years everyone had seemed fine with this.

By the time Helen had finished this thought process somehow the crumpet had been toasted, buttered and eaten. She hadn't even started Phil and Holly. Fuck it, she thought, reaching for another, if Will Smith had got fat, so could she. She wasn't going to see anyone for a while anyway. And certainly not on Friday.

Over the next two days Helen found herself looking out for any signs that this 'party' might actually be going to happen. Peeking past her blind occasionally, at Mrs Delgado's, she saw her doing the usual madness, sunbathing on a table, making what appeared to be new curtains from old pants. But nothing that looked like she was preparing an event.

The lack of chatter, or preparations, meant that by 6:55 on Friday night Helen was pretty certain this was going to be a quiet night. That if the flyers had gone out more widely, it had probably been shrugged off by the street as unnecessary and Mrs D had consequently lost interest. But just in case, Helen had a plan. Domino's delivery was booked for quarter-past (they had a no-contact policy on the pizzas from oven to customer and after research Helen has decided it was the safest takeaway option) and along with the food she had decided to watch a film called *Pitch Perfect*, which had been recommended by one of her old schoolfriends on Facebook. They said it was funny and cool and had singing.

All that was arranged, prepared, should have been great but at 6:55 Helen realised she was waiting. And she was anxious.

Why? Whatever happened would have nothing to do with her
so –

She heard the sound outside of a door opening, and voices.
She put her head round the blind, to look out on the street.
The occupants of the house opposite had come out. Three lads.
White, maybe students, young professionals (although Helen
felt they didn't look all that professional). One had a bag of
charcoal, another a small barbecue. The third was carrying a
crate of beer. They began to set up and as they did they made
loud man noises. Laughing in a way that echoed down the
street. Calling each other 'mate' and using words like
'awesome' and saying 'I guess' a lot. Helen never said 'I guess'.
No one her age did. That was a new, and Helen felt, unwelcome
Americanism. Anyway – Fine – she guessed they were going to
take part, but they looked the sort that would have done a
barbecue anyway. And anyway, it was just one house. Fine.

But then the door two-along opened and a woman wearing a
hijab came out. She was in her sixties and had with her a little
girl, who looked maybe six years old. Should probably have
been in bed by now. The woman was carrying a chair. The little
girl was carrying some juice cartons. The old woman smiled at
the three young men, one of whom called over to her

'Alright?'

'Yes thank you.' Said the old woman.

'Ready for this?'

'Oh yes.'

'Awesome.'

Helen was trying to work out if they knew each other. Not well,
but it wasn't the first time they'd spoken, clearly. They began to
have a conversation. The lads asked the little girl if she liked
burgers. She said she did and they said to the old woman she
could have one, if that was alright? They said they guessed it
was sharing food but no one would know and the burgers were
seriously lush, apparently. Corn-fed beef from Waitrose.

The old woman nodded thank you, it would be fine.

And so it begins, Helen thought. The great rule-bend. Not breaking the letter of the law but smashing the fucking hell out of the spirit.

Other doors were opening –– she could hear a swell of noise – people talking to each other, very loudly, leaning across. Passing things over.

And now, from down the street, holding a little trestle table and clutching a bag, appeared, Mrs Delgado. She was wearing the curtains she'd been making, but they weren't curtains they were some kind of strange red… thing, possibly an attempt at flamenco? And she had what looked like a crimson dahlia in her hair. On her feet were cowboy boots which didn't quite… well anyway – Dressed in her own style she made her way to the middle of the street and set up the trestle table. This she had practised, clearly, as it went up in seconds. Then from the bag she produced an old CD player and some CDs.

She looked up and smiled as someone said something to her. She was about to reply when –

No.

Helen moved away from the blind. It closed shut immediately. She didn't like any of this. Already she could hear people were shouting. They had booze, it was Friday night, it would only be a matter of time before they were getting closer – mixing. But this couldn't be her problem. She had a film to watch.

Suddenly with a creaking hinge, the noise from outside got louder. Oh no – Helen realised, clearly Tim, the bank clerk who lived in the flat downstairs, was in, had opened the front door to the building and was taking part.

Typical. Of course HE would think it was brilliant.

Helen put on the TV. *Channel 4 News*.

Turned it up.

There was a report from St Thomas's Hospital in London, which was close to being overwhelmed. People struggling to breathe. Ventilators. Distraught relatives telling the public to take care.

Outside she could still hear the laughing. She wondered... Was Mrs D right that there was in fact a thriving community the whole time that she didn't notice. Surely not but... Did people – like Mrs Delgado had suggested – know who she was? Surely not. Disinterested strangers in the city, right? That's the whole deal.

The noise had got quieter now and she could hear just one voice outside. The event, whatever it was, had started. She realised it was Mrs Delgado, she had her voice raised – she was – oh god she was making a speech. Wow. Introducing her entertainment. Whatever that was.

Helen went to Netflix and found the film – *Pitch Perfect*. She pressed play. As the idents started – in a sort of funny way – a kind of a capella version of the Universal music – it was discordantly interrupted by a loud man's opera voice outside starting up, singing the tune to football or ice creams. It sounded okay, she supposed, but she pitied the families with babies trying to –

Look –

Helen didn't want to be this person. Normally she was up for stuff. In normal times she actually would have quite liked a street party – she'd often said that maybe they should connect more – but come on!

Now?

Outside the opera had finished and now a Spanish guitar replaced it. It must've been playing through an amplifier as it was loud. She turned up the movie even more as the all-lady group took to the stage at the beginning – singing an Ace of Bass song. But all the tension of their appearance and the tunefulness of their singing was being destroyed by this Spanish guitar. So... she gave up. Paused the film. She couldn't watch it like this. And now it wasn't just a guitar, someone was singing in Spanish too, with a thick Spanish accent. God she hoped they were actually Spanish, or this was... awkward. A buzzer.

A buzzer?

Oh god – The pizza! She went to the intercom.

'Hello'

'Pizza'

'Yeah can you bring it up?'

'No I can't do that'

Sometimes they don't mind, but Helen understood.

'Okay. Hold on.'

She hung up the phone and put on her mask. Then she went down the stairs to the shared hallway where the front door was open. Just outside was the Domino's man, and Tim, in his banker's shirt, holding a bottle of beer. The Domino's man didn't see her. He was watching the tall, definitely-not-Spanish man singing and not even playing guitar in the middle of the road. The guitar was in fact a backing track, on Mrs Delgado's stereo.

'Hi' said Helen, and Domino's looked over.

'Oh hi.' He gave her the pizza from the bag, then turned back to the street. 'This is cool'

'Hmm' said Helen. 'Thanks'

He went to leave. Helen turned to go back upstairs.

'You not watching?'

Tim had called to her. She wondered if she had got far enough away to pretend she hadn't heard but decided not. Shit. She turned back.

'No. Quiet night in.'

'Tim. From downstairs.'

'Yes I know.'

'You want a beer? Got a pack.'

'Oh that's kind but I actually I was just going to – '

Helen stopped because Tim had broken out in a huge smile. He was looking at something on the street. Helen turned and saw Mrs Delgado beginning to dance, to the Spanish guitar music. Oh... Jeez. This explained the costume.

Her arms were up, her back straight. And she was…

I mean…

She was…

Well…

To be fair, she moved – given her age – with precision. Not fast, but elegant. With grace. Like she'd been trained at some point in her youth. The moves had… dignity. Poise. And the hubbub in the street, the laughing and chatter, it had all stopped as everyone had turned and watched Mrs Delgado, lit in the evening twilight under a street lamp, slowly and carefully… dancing.

Her head moved this way and that, part of the precision. She would approach different people and then retreat from them, as if flirting with the rules. Mocking them. She suddenly looked at Helen, right at her and her straight face broke and there was a flicker of what? Satisfaction? That Helen was here? Pleasure? That she had prevailed or was it just… joy?

Whatever it was for some reason Helen found herself moving forward. Taking step after step, drawn towards this old woman and these – movements. The music was building – a crescendo of Spanish passion it should be ridiculous here in the street but somehow the incongruity made one look closer, and made the dance somehow mesmerising, to everyone there. Everyone in the street, was just staring, watching, as she –

Click.

It all stopped. Suddenly.

Mrs Delgado jerked, surprised out of the moment, then looked up.

Helen had turned off the stereo.

'What are you doing?'

'You need to stop.'

'Why?'

'Why would you organise this? After everything I've been saying. Do you not understand?'

People were coming over, looking annoyed, aggressively heading towards Helen. 'What's going on? What happened? What you doing love, didn't you see that?'

She backed away.

'Stop.'

'What's she doing?'

'It's alright' said Mrs Delgado. But Helen told them –

'Stay away stay away from me all of you you shouldn't be out here you shouldn't be touching and coming close and near her and old people and sharing food and drinks, and some of you were hugging, do you understand what this is? If you care about the community, if you really do, you should stop this, just stop.'

Some of them took a step back, a little caught out –

'We're all being careful.'

'You're not.'

'Who are you anyway?'

'Helen. She lives over there.' Said Mrs Delgado. 'She means well.'

'I...'

Helen was outraged.

'Means well? Uh yes uh I do I do fucking I do fucking mean well' said Helen, 'but more than that I *do* well I do my best not like the rest of you, you talk about community talk about looking after each other but that's not what this is about this is just about trying to have a party so you have a good time but it won't mean that in six months any of you are actually *there* for each other, you won't sacrifice anything for each other, you think this is going to *change* things and bring us *together* it will not, because – right – you know the amazing thing about lockdown is not how hard it was to live without other people for

months and months and months but how fucking easy we found
it, really, and actually that's not surprising because that's
exactly what companies want us to do isn't it, even at the best
of times, monetise every interaction, make sure we don't share
but we buy our own, that we don't repair that we replace, that
we don't talk we type and not much of that, and if we do talk
that we do it on their networks their phones, that we don't
seduce we swipe, we've been trained to be separate from each
other because that's how they make money so compared to even
twenty years ago we're all in *permanent* lockdown anyway and
if you want to actually, genuinely, *connect* like probably people
should, like that would make life worth living you're fighting
all of that all the billions spent on building commercialised
atomised fucking walls put up to pile pressure on us to aspire
and compete to squeeze as much work out of us, and to make us
spend all the fucking time. We're learning the wrong lesson, we
shouldn't *want* it to get back to *normal* – you really want to
make a community? We should stay home, stay alive till this
passes then the moment we're all vaccinated, if that day ever
comes we should go into the street, collectively destroy our
phones, plant a fucking garden, share everything, make things
not buy things and sit not with beer for an evening but with *food*
for hours every day every evening of our lives and share it all
and everyone knows all the evidence shows that would make us
happier healthier richer in the real sense of the word and the
climate would be better and the only thing that would suffer
would be Amazon.com but they don't pay tax anyway so they
can fuck off that's why I'm here because this is all wrong in so
many ways, not just because it's against the rules but because
it's fake and nonsense cos you're not going to do any of what I
just said because you're not really prepared to sacrifice anything
of your lifestyle are you? To really SHARE?? Any of you.

Even just say you won't use Amazon. Can you do that? Cos
they are really SHIT.

Can you do that?

I can't.

I can't even stop doing fucking that.

Or eating. I eat all the time.'

They stared at her.

'But at least I don't pretend I'm helping.

At least I don't pretend I'm good.

You don't know what a community is you you you – '

She caught her breath.

She was still holding the Domino's pizza box under her arm. Which she realised undermined the quite radical anti-capitalist things she was saying but...

She felt sick.

'Let's um...'

Mrs Delgado spoke quietly. Everyone turned to her.

'Let's call it a night. Just enjoy your evenings everyone. Alright?'

After a brief pause, there was some nodding and people dispersed. A few muttered 'shames'. Mrs Delgado stood opposite Helen, who for some reason didn't move. Found she couldn't move. Just stood there with the pizza.

Mrs D looked at her. She didn't look back.

'This is hard, isn't it?' said Mrs Delgado.

A moment. Helen unsure.

Then she said.

'There's nothing wrong with me'

'I know'

'I'm not mad. Depressed. Whatever.'

'No'

'I'm right'

'Yes you are'

'What?'

'That was very honest and very true'

Helen finally looked up at Mrs D. They just stared at each other.

Helen was about to turn away, take her pizza and head back in, to lukewarm Domino's and *Pitch Perfect* on Netflix watched at a forty-five-degree angle but just before she broke eye contact Mrs Delgado said

'Helen. I know what you've been saying. I understand. It doesn't come easily to me. It's not in my nature. But if I try. If I promise you, from now on, that I'll follow the rules, will you do something for me?'

Helen sighed. Looked at the ground. She was tired. She wanted cold pizza. But if this last piece of madness was the cost of getting home... She looked back up.

'What?' She asked

'Well I've been trying to hint at this for a while but it's not communicated obviously and forgive me if I seem stilted it's not usual for me to need to spell things out but anyway... Helen:

'Will you be my friend?'

Helen couldn't believe this. Seriously... how old were they? *'Will you be my friend?'*

'I'll happily give Amazon up. I don't like it anyway'

What was she – Oh oh! Helen's face filled with blood and panic what the fuck what the fuckety fucking shit fuck fuck?? She was going to have to – no too late it's happened she was crying.

'Shit.'

Sniffing, wobbling teary proper messy street crying with any attempt to cover not being helped by having one arm out of action hugging a Domino's. Shit. She took a step back.

'Don't worry I'm not going to hug you.'

'Good' said Helen.

Helen used her sleeve to deal with the fluids the best she could

'I'm not going to offer you a tissue either'

'Right' said Helen

'See?' said Mrs D

'What?' said Helen.

'I'm learning.'

'Oh. Yeah.'

A moment. Then Helen said –

'Yes'

'Sorry?' said Mrs Delgado.

'Yes' said Helen, 'this is hard. All of this. Really hard.'

They stood for a moment.

And Helen looked at Mrs Delgado and realised that maybe them clashing was actually them getting on. That in their case, at least, they required something of the opposite: Helen needed help to sometimes step over the line. Mrs Delgado needed help to realise there was one. Maybe after all this, yes, they could be friends.

And Mrs Delgado looked at Helen and knew she was a good person who was probably in fact right about the Covid laws and seemed quite strait-laced but, as was clear through the blind a long time ago, was secretly quite radical, maybe they would get on, and maybe as a bonus she might still have access to drugs. Either way, in the end, life was simple: If someone's in trouble, you help.

And if Helen really wanted to start a hippy anti-capitalist commune, as she seemed to be indicating in her strange outburst, then April Delgado would be first in the door.

And they stood, next to each other, apart.

But for the first time, together.

And from across the road I watched. And wondered who they were.

PHOENIX

Phoenix was first produced by ETT as part of Signal Fires, a national storytelling project. The story was read by Bertie Carvel, directed by Richard Twyman, with sound design and composition by Ben and Max Ringham.

He shouldn't be here, Tim thought, as he stood in the dark,
throwing plastic wrapper after plastic wrapper into the designer
fire pit. He could hear behind him the muffled sound of his two-
year-old daughter crying, and his wife of five years trying to get
her to sleep. He had said there was a phone call to make and
had escaped but that was a lie. He had needed a moment to
himself, so he had gone to the car, grabbed the packet of
Cadbury's Celebrations from the glove compartment and
headed back to the designer fire pit where up until an hour ago
they had been sat drinking wine. He'd stoked it and thankfully
it had come back to life, the last couple of logs still with some
flame. Since the birth of their child he had given up his vices.
He drank in extreme moderation. He didn't smoke any more.
Drugs were years ago. But he could still eat chocolate. And then
he realised if he threw the plastic onto the fire he could smell
the mildly toxic fumes that came out. And he liked that. The
idea of doing something very slightly wrong.

But of course he was doing something more than very slightly
wrong in this moment. That was the problem. He felt sick, deep
in his stomach. He thought this must be what it feels like when
someone has committed murder but no one else knows yet. Or
stolen something extremely valuable. Like when the crime has
been committed but the other shoe is yet to drop. The shit yet to
hit the fan. And only you know. Only the culprit is aware,
through this sickness, that they are in the calm before the storm.

He stopped eating the chocolates. He wasn't hungry. Instead he
just took the wrappers off and kept burning them.

He wished he had a fucking cigarette.

The sound of his daughter, still crying. And across the way, he
could hear a television on in the big house. His parents were
watching *Downtown Abbey*. Not for the first time. His little
family were staying in 'The Stable', a converted outhouse on

his parents' smallholding. They'd had it a few years. It was tasteful, but soulless. Much like them.

His phone was filling up with emails every minute, but that was normal. If that stopped, then he'd really be worried.

How had he ended up in this situation? It all felt so... pathetic. And without influence. Buffeted by circumstances when he had spent his adult life telling everyone who'd listen, student societies, then campaign groups, think tanks and now the highest level of government, that one must always act strategically. Take the time and press forward with what you want. You start trying to fix things, address problems, soothe, apologise, solve, salve or explain and you'll weaken. Sink. You'll never escape.

And yet that was exactly what he had done in the last twelve hours. He'd only reacted, spontaneously and impulsively and as a result had made a number of terrible decisions. All leading him here to this fucking designer fire pit.

And now his imagination was starting to work. This was almost certainly going to be the end for him. And his career, and his family. When the people found out that he had contravened the rules, the guidance, possibly even the law (was it the law yet? He had to find out) to come up here, they'd have what they needed to remove him. They wouldn't care that in these circumstances the list of people his wife would allow to look after their daughter was four people long and that two of those people were her parents who lived in New Zealand. And that him and his wife were looking like with this positive diagnosis they might get very ill indeed and so it really was their only option to get to his parents as quickly as they could. No one would hear that. Or believe it. And as he sat there he didn't think it sounded much more than an excuse. Others will, at this moment, be dealing with worse...

Why did he agree with her? She just went on and on at him. Saying there was no option saying he had to put his daughter first this time to hell with anything else this was family and if he didn't drive them she'd get in the fucking car and do it herself, and he tried to make an argument but she didn't listen, she wasn't rational she was just thinking about herself and their daughter and nothing else.

Which, he supposed, is what a parent is supposed to do.

In which case what was he? As throughout it all, he was thinking of all sorts of things. They could get an emergency nanny. They had friends. It would all be fine. And the consequences of breaking the rules could be disastrous, for the future. For the career.

But she had kept on. And he... he'd found himself getting their stuff in the car in half an hour then them all getting in and setting off up north, only calling his parents once they were on their way... How had he made that decision? He found he couldn't remember...

His wife appeared at the window looking for him. He sent a text to her. 'Sorry this is taking a while.' She received it and looked irritated. He hated her for a split second. She had put on weight since the baby, but he had got fitter. She was greying. His hair was thick and dark.

They were heading in different directions as they got older, he was realising. He was getting more attractive, she was getting less. And she'd developed this hectoring tone...

Was that why he'd done it? He'd simply capitulated to her going on and on, like a downtrodden husband from an eighties sitcom.

He thought of the last woman he'd had sex with before he met his wife. In 2014. She was thirty. A hotel receptionist in New York. She'd flirted with him, and at first he thought it was just her professional manner, but day by day she'd become more forward and he'd responded. By the end of the week they were having a drink on her night off. He'd ended booking the best suite in the hotel. It had cost him a month's salary but it was worth every penny. They'd drank and kissed and smoked on the roof overlooking the city, then taken each other's clothes off and fucking fucked in all sorts of ways until they were sweaty and made such a huge mess. They had woken early, showered and gone for breakfast at a terrible diner then walked in the autumn leaves in Central Park. At the time he hadn't known it was a last hurrah. But... hurrah.

A far cry from this. In the grip. Of a situation. Of a wife. A child. A role. A global fucking pandemic at the worst possible fucking moment. Just when he was getting everything done.

He looked out into the dark. What if he just walked away. He could simply start again. That would be wonderfully strategic. Convention would tell you there would be huge consequences. There wouldn't. He could find new low-profile work. He could deal with his soon-to-be ex-wife and child via intermediaries and emails. His friends would be shocked but the important ones would stick by him, putting it down to a mid-life crisis. His daughter would hate him, but there were millions of daughters who hated their fathers. And who knows, she might eventually understand it and they would have a relationship. And he would be free. To do whatever the fuck he wanted again. To change the world. To change HIS world.

The darkness. Out there. It appealed. He threw the Celebrations box on the fire. It burned quickly and disappeared.

To be honest he might have to escape soon anyway. After what he'd done, cajoled into this foolish trip, he would be forced to resign and everything he was trying to achieve in government would be at an end. And more than that, he was such a high-profile figure that his disobeyance of the rules might lead to a national collapse in confidence in the government's response. And that collapse could lead to people NOT following the rules, and that would, as things were right now, lead to deaths. Thousands of deaths. And yes the more he thought about it the more he realised there was no escaping that reality. When this emerged, as it no doubt would, he, and his nagging wife, would have been responsible for more people dead than would fit in a sports hall. Thousands maybe. What would that do to him? That would be all that his life would be about. This mistake. And the consequences.

The unmistakable tone of Carson complaining. His daughter now calming down.

His wife singing her to sleep.

A crackling fire starting to die.

He went over to the log store. It was empty. He went back to the fire then looked around. There was a tree in the dark. He had no torch and so stumbled across the field towards it. His foot hit a – what? – maybe a clump, and he tripped and fell into the dirt. He lay there for a second, enjoying the cool of the ground, enjoying lying down; the simplicity of the earth.

Perhaps he could just stay here and see what happened?

He hauled himself to his feet and staggered over to the tree. He ran his hands on the ground, around the trunk and found dry material. Not branches but a lot of twigs, protected from the rain by the canopy of leaves above. He picked some up in his hands but it wasn't enough. It would be gone quickly and he was enjoying the fucking fire. He looked back at it – it was nearly dead, nearly gone forever.

Strategy.

He took off his jumper suddenly, leaving him only in a thin T-shirt. He knotted the sleeves and the hole for his head and made a bag out of it, then he started filling it with dry twigs. When he'd finished, he started back towards the fire, but the flames looked so small and nearly gone so he ran. He ran, covered in mud and wet, holding his jumper bag, and as soon as he got back to the embers he tipped the twigs onto the last few flames. As he did it, dust went up on the air, and in a moment he realised he'd made a mistake. The tipping of the twigs had crushed the embers, stopped the oxygen and put the whole thing out.

He was desperate. Once again, he hadn't been thinking. What had happened to him?

Whatever the unique talent was that had got him this far, had gone. He'd made a series of mistakes and his life had led him to a child he didn't love, a wife who disgusted him, a cold field and thousands dead, at his hands.

He shut his eyes…

…then suddenly he felt the heat. He opened them and saw the fire burst back, as the twigs finally caught, and it burned brightly, more than ever before.

He sat. The fire hot, and captivating.

His wife had come to the window, noticing the flames. She had a cup of tea now and as the yellow light caught her face she looked beautiful. So much more sexual and wonderful and intelligent than that fucking hotel girl. This was the woman he loved. And she didn't nag, she fought. For their child. And that wasn't wrong. That was primal.

And now he remembered! He hadn't been nagged into the decision, there had been a moment, as he began to pack up provisions in their kitchen before they left, that he'd realised this was completely the right thing to do. Put his family first and figure it out from there. He would tell anyone else to do the same. And he was strong, he was literally in power, this was the right thing to do and he would deal with the consequences.

And as the flames danced he made a new plan. No one knew about this trip currently. Not really. He would keep it that way. Not hidden exactly but unremarkable. And if eventually it came out, he would be unapologetic. He did the right thing for his family. He was an important man doing important things. He felt certainty in his core. There was absolutely one rule for him and one rule for them. Because he wasn't like them. He was exceptional, in the factual use of the word. He had got to where he was because he was not like the rest. And maybe there would be thousands dead on this occasion but because of his work, his interventions, his policies, his determination and courage, many more would live and thrive and not many individuals had the guts to deal with those calculations and take on leadership of scale and existence but it was necessary that some people did and he was well qualified to be one of those few.

He stood up, now warm and bright, and ready to return to the house.

Fuck them all. He could do what he wanted. Because he was right. Sooner or later they would realise that. And if they hated him in the meantime he would just smile.

He wife saw him through the window, and looked surprised. She smiled at him. Like she saw him in a new way. Like he must look newly attractive. Sexy maybe.

Their daughter had gone to sleep. The evening was young. He smiled at his wife and started to head back to the house, feeling elemental, powerful and very much in control. He was ready.

His wife opened the door and they kissed. Tonight would be glorious. As he had told his colleagues for years...

There was an opportunity in any crisis.

A Nick Hern Book

Mrs Delgado first published in Great Britain in 2021 as a paperback original by Nick Hern Books Limited, The Glasshouse, 49a Goldhawk Road, London W12 8QP, in association with the Old Fire Station, Oxford

Mrs Delgado copyright © 2021 Mike Bartlett
Phoenix copyright © 2021 Mike Bartlett

Mike Bartlett has asserted his right to be identified as the author of this work

Cover design by Rebecca Pitt

Designed and typeset by Nick Hern Books, London
Printed in Great Britain by Mimeo Ltd, Huntingdon, Cambridgeshire PE29 6XX

A CIP catalogue record for this book is available from the British Library

ISBN 978 1 83904 054 2